S0-BRA-208

Autumn
LEAVES FALL FROM THE TREES!

By LISA BELL

Illustrated by EMILY BROOKS

CANTATA
LEARNING

MANKATO, MINNESOTA

WWW.CANTATALEARNING.COM

CANTATA
LEARNING
MANKATO, MINNESOTA

Published by Cantata Learning
1710 Roe Crest Drive
North Mankato, MN 56003
www.cantatalearning.com

Library of Congress Control Number: 2014956854
978-1-63290-260-3 (hardcover/CD)
978-1-63290-412-6 (paperback/CD)
978-1-63290-454-6 (paperback)

Autumn: Leaves Fall from the Trees! by Lisa Bell
Illustrated by Emily Brooks

Book design, Tim Palin Creative
Editorial direction, Flat Sole Studio
Executive musical production and direction, Elizabeth Draper
Music arranged and produced by Mark Oblinger

Printed in the United States of America.

VISIT
WWW.CANTATALEARNING.COM/ACCESS-OUR-MUSIC
TO SING ALONG TO THE SONG

Fall is the season between summer and winter. It is also called autumn. Many changes happen during this time of year. Leaves change color and fall from the trees. The weather turns cooler. Snow may even fall!

Now turn the page, and sing along.

Leaves fall from the trees.

There's a **crisp**, cool breeze.

Go out and play!

It's a fine fall day.

There's now a chill in the air.
We take our time to dress with care.

We make sure that we are warm
in case the weather starts to storm.

Autumn leaves fall when the wind blows.

The yard fills with reds and yellows.

We rake a pile, and when we're done,

we dive right in and have some fun!

Leaves fall from the trees.

There's a crisp, cool breeze.

Go out and play!

It's a fine fall day.

Farmers work to pick their crops
before the **temperature** really drops.

Carrots, squash, and turnips too
will make a tasty autumn **stew**.

We pick pumpkins from the vine.
Soon we will have pumpkin pie.

And above it all are flying geese,
migrating south in a *V*.

Pick red, **ripe** apples low and high
to gather for a perfect pie.

The kitchen's full of smells **galore**.
Cinnamon, spice, and so much more!

19

Leaves fall from the trees.

There's a crisp, cool breeze.

Go out and play!

It's a fine fall day.

SONG LYRICS
Autumn: Leaves Fall from the Trees!

Leaves fall from the trees.
There's a crisp, cool breeze.

Go out and play!
It's a fine fall day.

There's now a chill in the air.
We take our time to dress with care.

We make sure that we are warm
in case the weather starts to storm.

Autumn leaves fall when the wind
   blows.
The yard fills with reds and yellows.

We rake a pile, and when we're done,
we dive right in and have some fun!

Leaves fall from the trees.
There's a crisp, cool breeze.

Go out and play!
It's a fine fall day.

Farmers work to pick their crops
before the temperature really drops.

Carrots, squash, and turnips too
will make a tasty autumn stew.

We pick pumpkins from the vine.
Soon we will have pumpkin pie.

And above it all are flying geese,
migrating south in a *V*.

Pick red, ripe apples low and high
to gather for a perfect pie.

The kitchen's full of smells galore.
Cinnamon, spice, and so much more!

Leaves fall from the trees.
There's a crisp, cool breeze.

Go out and play!
It's a fine fall day.

Autumn: Leaves Fall from the Trees!

Chorus

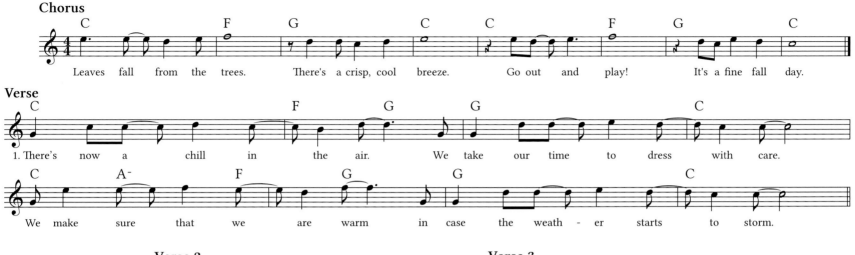

Leaves fall from the trees. There's a crisp, cool breeze. Go out and play! It's a fine fall day.

Verse

1. There's now a chill in the air. We take our time to dress with care. We make sure that we are warm in case the weath-er starts to storm.

Verse 2

Autumn leaves fall when the wind blows.
The yard fills with reds and yellows.
We rake a pile, and when we're done,
we dive right in and have some fun!

Chorus

Leaves fall from the trees.
There's a crisp, cool breeze.
Go out and play!
It's a fine fall day.

Verse 3

Farmers work to pick their crops
before the temperature really drops.
Carrots, squash, and turnips too
will make a tasty autumn stew.

Verse 4

We pick pumpkins from the vine.
Soon we will have pumpkin pie.
And above it all are flying geese,
migrating south in a V.

Bridge

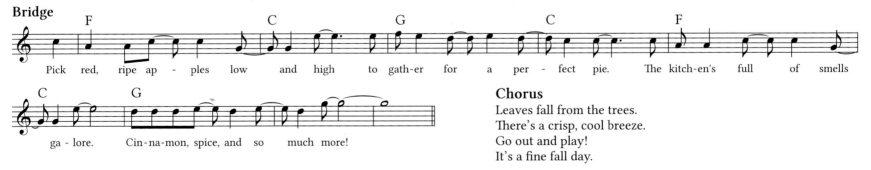

Pick red, ripe ap-ples low and high to gath-er for a per-fect pie. The kitch-en's full of smells ga-lore. Cin-na-mon, spice, and so much more!

Chorus

Leaves fall from the trees.
There's a crisp, cool breeze.
Go out and play!
It's a fine fall day.

GLOSSARY

crisp—cool and fresh

galore—in large numbers

migrating—moving from one place to another, usually to find food as the seasons change

ripe—ready to pick and eat

stew—a food made with vegetables and meat and cooked slowly for a long time

temperature—the measure of how hot or cold something is

GUIDED READING ACTIVITIES

1. What is this story mostly about?

2. What are some facts from the story? What are opinions?

3. Do you have a favorite fall activity? What is it, and why do you enjoy it?

TO LEARN MORE

Cocca-Leffler, Maryann. *Let It Fall*. New York: Cartwheel Books, 2010.

DeGezelle, Terri. *Exploring Fall*. North Mankato, MN: Capstone, 2012.

Holland, Loretta. *Fall Leaves*. New York: Houghton Mifflin-Harcourt, 2014.

Smith, Siân. *What Can You See in Fall?* Chicago, IL: Capstone-Heinemann, 2015.